THE CHAFING DISH SPECIALTIES

OF THE
WORLD FAMOUS CHEFS

UNITED STATES
CANADA
EUROPE

Compiled and Edited by
A. C. HOFF

Creative Cookbooks
Monterey, California

The Chafing Dish Specialties of the World Famous Chefs:
United States, Canada, Europe

Compiled and Edited by
A. C. Choff

ISBN: 1-4101-0319-6

Copyright © 2003 by Fredonia Books

Reprinted from the 1913 edition

Creative Cookbooks
An Imprint of Fredonia Books
Monterey, California
http://www.creativecookbooks.com

All rights reserved, including the right to reproduce this book, or portions thereof, in any form.

In order to make original editions of historical works available to scholars at an economical price, this facsimile of the original edition of 1913 is reproduced from the best available copy and has been digitally enhanced to improve legibility, but the text remains unaltered to retain historical authenticity.

CONTRIBUTORS

Emile Bailly, Chef	Hotel St. Regis	New York City
Jean S. Berdou, Chef	Hotel Astor	New York City
Jean Millon, Chef	Ritz-Carlton	New York City
Henry Berger, Chef	Frankfurter-Hof	Frankfurt, German
Jules Kohler, Chef	Hotel Adlon	Berlin, Germany
G. Milhau, Chef	Tait-Zinkand Cafe	San Francisco
Adrian Delvaux, Chef	Hotel Baltimore	Kansas City
Otto Geutsch, Chef	Hotel Windsor	Montreal
Joseph D. Campazzi, Chef	Royal Poinciana	Palm Beach
E. C. Perault, Chef	Planters Hotel	St. Louis
John Chiappano, Chef	Auditorium Hotel	Chicago
Geo. R. Meyer, Chef	Rector's Cafe	Chicago
Gerard Embregts, Chef	Chateau Frontenac	Quebec
Louis Pfaff, Chef	New Willard Hotel	Washington
Henry Johannsen, Chef	Hotel Royal Palm	Miami
Victor Hirtzler, Chef	Hotel St. Francis	San Francisco
Emile Burgermeister, Chef	Hotel Fairmont	San Francisco
Martin Ginder, Chef	Hotel Green	Pasadena
Joseph Stoltz, Chef	Hotel Ponce de Leon	St. Augustine
Henri Boutroue, Chef	Hotel Shelbourne	Dublin, Ireland
Thos. Cooney, Chef	Van Nuys Hotel	Los Angeles
Jules Dauviller, Chef	Palace Hotel	San Francisco
Arthur Taylor, Chef	Hotel Raymond	Pasadena
Ernest Otzenberger, Chef	Hotel Dennis	Atlantic City
Cesar Obrecht, Chef	Grand Hotel de L'Europe	Lucerne, Switzerland
Jules Boucher, Chef	Arlington Hotel	Hot Springs
Chas. Grolimund, Chef	Washington Hotel	Seattle
Jean Juillard, Chef	Hotel Adolphus	Dallas
Chas. Pier Giorgi, Chef	Hotel Alcazar	St. Augustine
Peter Bona, Chef	Hotel Chamberlain	Fortress Monroe
Louis Lescarboura, Chef	Ft. Pitt Hotel	Pittsburgh
John Pfaff, Chef	Hotel Cape May	Cape May
Walter Jurenz, Chef	Hotel Galvez	Galveston
S. B. Pettengill, Chef	Hotel Ormond	Ormond Beach
Geo. E. Schaff, Chef	Hotel Albany	Denver
Ben E. Dupaquier, Chef	Hotel Arlington	Santa Barbara
William Leon Benzeni, Chef	Hotel Virginia	Long Beach
Chas. A. Frey, Chef	Hotel Alexandria	Los Angeles
Lucien Fusier, Chef	Grand Hotel Metropole	Interlaken, Switzerland
G. Cloux, Chef	U. S. Grant Hotel	San Diego
A. Schloettke, Chef	Westminster Hotel	Dresden, Germany
Lucien Raymond, Chef	Hotel Congress & Annex	Chicago
Louis Thein, Chef	Hotel Utah	Salt Lake City
Jules Edward Bole, Chef	Hotel Jefferson	St. Louis
John Bicochi, Chef	Hotel Piedmont	Atlanta
Edw. R. J. Fischel, Steward	Hotel Piedmont	Atlanta,
Leopold Saux, Steward	Hotel Grunewald	New Orleans
Henri D. Fouilloux, Steward	St. Charles Hotel	New Orleans

WORLD RENOWNED HOTELS

Their Chefs—Our Contributors

WORLD RENOWNED HOTELS

Their Chefs—Our Contributors

PREFACE

In presenting to the public this book on CHAFING DISH SPECIALTIES we feel that we are presenting the most complete authoritative and up-to-date book ever prepared on the subject. The contributors being the finest chefs in the United States, Canada and Europe insure every recipe shown as right. These world famous chefs have given us their special recipes and they have made the explanations so plain and so complete that any one can readily understand them.

The great chefs who have prepared these recipes for us have all made cooking their life work and have been apprenticed under the finest and most practical teachers in the culinary lines in this country and abroad.

A large portion of the copy has been translated from the French. The finest chefs are generally the French or Swiss. They are not literary men; their language is not flowery, but we know that even with the difficulty that exists in expressing in English many of the French terms that the work as a whole will be easily understood and greatly appreciated.

This is the first time in history that such a wonderful collection of recipes have been made obtainable for general use. These men are giving, in these recipes, their "professional secrets." The calibre of the men who have prepared these recipes is great and represents as much as the great masters in other lines of the world's work. Napoleon Bonaparte was a great general; Shakespeare, a great author; George Washington, a wonderful statesman; and Thomas Edison, a masterful inventor:—but we feel that the master chefs represented here are to be considered just as great and doing just as much of the world's work as any of the famous men we have all been taught to revere and respect.

The International Cooking Library, covering in ten volumes, every conceivable part, section or angle of the cooking question makes it possible for any one who will follow these recipes to be an expert cook. The great masters who have prepared these recipes have spent their

Their Chefs—Our Contributors

lives studying and experimenting and are giving in these recipes their best ideas and suggestions. These are dishes of the millionaires and the most particular epicureans.

We feel that this set of books is presented to the public at just the opportune time. All people are beginning to realize that there is really no more important art than cooking and this should be so; for what should be considered more important than what we eat? The best health insurance is having the right kind of foods, properly prepared. A man is at his best only when he is in robust health and nothing will undermine a person's constitution so quickly as poor food. The best dishes and the sure and absolute recipes for making them, are contained in this wonderful set of books. All the copy is from authorities just as positive and just as sure in this line as the noted Blackstone was on legal lines. We picked the best chefs in the world; we would accept copy from no others.

A careful study of the recipes and careful application of the directions for same is all that is necessary to produce the results that have made these men famous.

In the presentation of this book, we wish only that space would allow us to mention and pay courtesy to the many men who have assisted us in the various departments, copy preparation, translation, and editing, also the courtesies rendered by the managers of the world renowned hotels whose chefs have been our contributors.

INTERNATIONAL PUBLISHING COMPANY

WORLD RENOWNED HOTELS

INDEX

CHAFING DISH SPECIALTIES

PAGE

EMILE BAILLY, Chef de Cuisine, HOTEL ST. REGIS, New York, N. Y............ 12
    CRAB MEAT AND OYSTERS A LA A. C. HOFF
    CRUISSES DES GRENOUILLES POULETTE
    CHICKEN A LA KING
    EMINCEE DE RIZ DE VEAU FINANCIER

GEO. R. MEYER, Chef de Cuisine, RECTOR'S CAFE, Chicago, Ill................ 13
    CHICKEN LYDIA   SAUCE SUPREME
    LOBSTER NEWBERG   LOBSTER ABINITIO
    CRAB MEAT NORFOLK

JOHN PFAFF, Chef de Cuisine, HOTEL CAPE MAY, Cape May, N. J............ 21
    CRAB FLAKES, NEWBERG   CHICKEN A LA KING
    SWEETBREAD A LA HOTEL CHAMPLAIN

JOSEPH STOLTZ, Chef de Cuisine, PONCE DE LEON HOTEL, St. Augustine, Fla. 22
    FROG LEGS   SWEETBREADS
    SQUAB CHICKEN

MARTIN GINDER, Chef de Cuisine, HOTEL GREEN, Pasadena, Cal...... 24
    SHAD ROE SAUTE   SCRAMBLED EGGS
    OYSTER CREAM SAUCE   WELSH RAREBIT GOURMANT
    MINCED CHICKEN A LA GREEN LOBSTER

HENRY JOHANNSEN, Chef de Cuisine, HOTEL ROYAL PALM, Miami, Fla..... 26
    LOBSTER, ARISTOCRAT   CAPON, BIGARURE
    MELI, "MELO" ROYAL PALACE

CHAS. A. FREY, Chef de Cuisine, HOTEL ALEXANDRIA, Los Angeles, Ca 27
    CRAB A LA CLEOPATRE   SLICES OF CAPON FORESTIERE

WILLIAM LEON BENZENI, Chef de Cuisine, HOTEL VIRGINIA, Long Beach, Cal. 28
    PLANKED CROWN OF MILK LAMB
    REED BIRD A LA PAUL LECOURT
    FILET OF STRIPED BASS A LA C. STANLEY
    TOMATO FRICASSEE IN A CHAFING DISH
    FLANKED SHAD DINNER A LA MAYOR STOY
    LOBSTER A LA AMERICAINE
    SPAGHETTI FOR LUNCHEON
    ROAST SQUAB CHICKEN A LA LENA FRANK

E. C. PERAULT, Chef de Cuisine, PLANTERS HOTEL, St. Louis, Mo............ 31
    CHICKEN SPECIAL   SEAFOODS
    SWEETBREADS A LA PLANTERS

LOUIS LESCARBOURA, Chef de Cuisine, FORT PITT HOTEL, Pittsburg, Pa..... 34
    CRAB FLAKES SUBLIME   CHAFING DISH PEPITA
    CHAFING DISH KNICKERBOCKER

JULES DAUVILLER, Chef de Cuisine, PALACE HOTEL, San Francisco, Cal....... 32
    SCRAMBLED EGGS MAJOR RATHBONE   RISDE'VEAU PALACE
    CRAB FLAKES A LA KING   FROG LEGS CHINJARADA

Their Chefs—Our Contributors

HENRI FOUILLOUX, Chef de Cuisine, HOTEL ST. CHARLES, New Orleans, La.. 35
   IMPERIAL STEW   BREAST OF MALLARD DUCK AU PORTO

LOUIS PFAFF, Chef de Cuisine, NEW WILLARD HOTEL, Washington, D.C...... 36
   LOBSTER MEXICAINE   TERRAPIN
   CHICKEN A LA KING   CRAB FLAKES A LA DEWEY

EMILE BURGERMEISTER, Chef de Cuisine, FAIRMONT HOTEL, San Francisco, 37
   CRAB FLAKES MADRAS   OYSTER AND FROG LEGS, FAIRMONT
   FROG LEGS DUGLEVA   LOBSTER GOURMANT
   MUSHROOMS IN RED WINE PEACH FLAMBEES
   SQUAB CHICKEN NELSON   SWEETBREADS LORRAINE
           POACHED EGG MILANNAISE

VICTOR HIRTZLER, Chef de Cuisine, HOTEL ST. FRANCIS, San Francisco, Cal. 16
   EGGS BECHAMEL   FINNAN HADDIE
   FROG LEGS MICHELS   SWEET BREADS MONZA
   FONDUE SAVARIN   FINNAN HADDIE IN CREAM
   CREAMED FINNAN HADDIE CRAB MEAT IN CREAM
   CRAB MEAT MONZA   CRAB MEAT GOURMANT
   TERRAPIN MARYLAND   TERRAPIN JOCKEY CLUB
   TERRAPIN BALTIMORE   CURRIED CRAB
   SHRIMP WITH MUSHROOMS CRAB IN CHAFING DISH
       FROGS A LA POULETTE
       SLICED FILLET OF BEEF A L' ESTRAGON
       OYSTERS OR CRAB A LA POULETTE

OTTO GEUTSCH, Chef de Cuisine, WINDSOR HOTEL, Montreal, Canada........ 40
        GRENOUILLES SENORITA
        EMINCE DE VOLAILLE ANNA HELD
        ROGNONS D' AGNEAU MARCHAN VIN
        EMINCE DE RIS DE VEAU MIKADO

JULES EDWARD BOLE, Chef de Cuisine, JEFFERSON HOTEL, St. Louis, Mo... 42
   CAPON AND LOBSTER NEPTUNE   HUITRES EN OMBRELLE
   MINCED CHICKEN JEFFERSON   RAGOUT FIN QUATRE SEASON
        GRENOUILLE ET CRAB GRENOBLOISE

PETER BONA, Chef de Cuisine, HOTEL CHAMBERLIN, Fortress, Monroe, Va... 41
      SWEETBREADS A LA BILL EN CHAFING DISH
      FRESH CRAB FLAKES A LA ADAMS
      ESCALLOPS D CAPON A LA BONA

ADRIAN DELVAUX, Chef de Cuisine, HOTEL BALTIMORE' Kansas City, Mo... 43
      MINCED CHICKEN BALTIMORE IN CHAFING DISH
      LOBSTER BALTIMORE IN CHAFING DISH
      CRAB MEAT BALTIMORE IN CHAFING DISH

JOHN CHIAPPANO, Chef de Cuisine, AUDITORIUM HOTEL, Chicago, Ill....... 47
      EMINCE OF CHICKEN A LA AUDITORIUM
      SWEETBREADS SANS JENE
      FROG LEGS A LA NICOLO DEILAPI
      LOBSTER MERRY WIDOW

ARTHUR TAYLOR, Chef de Cuisine, HOTEL RAYMOND, Pasadena, Cal........ 45
      VENISON STEAK
      MUSSELS A LA MARINIERE EN CHAFING DISH

BEN. E. DUPAQUIER, Chef de Cuisine, HOTEL ARLINGTON, Santa Barbara, Cal. 46
      VEAL SWEETBREADS AND FRESH MUSHROOMS A LA DUNN
      LOBSTER A LA ARLINGTON

WORLD FAMOUS CHEFS

EMILE BAILLY,
CHEF DE CUISINE
HOTEL ST. REGIS
New York City, N.Y.
Mr. Bailly prior to coming to this country served in the very best hotels in Europe. He left the Grand Hotel of Monte Carlo, France ten years ago, to come to New York and open the St. Regis.

CHAIR DE CRAB AND HUITRES A LA A. C. HOFF
CRAB MEAT AND OYSTERS, A LA A. C. HOFF

(A Specialty of the St. Regis Hotel, by Mr. E. Bailly, Chef, in honor of Mr. A. C. Hoff.)

Take ten ounces of boiled crab meat and cream it; have the sauce very white; also one dozen oysters poached in butter, add a little thickening. Strain the sauce through linen and finish off with spinach butter. On the other hand peel and select two nice ripe tomatoes, cut in dice without mashing them too much. Put same on a butter spread platter, salt and pepper and put in oven, drain off before serving. The last minute garnish a chafing dish by placing the crab meat in first, the tomatoes in the center and the oysters well dipped in spinach butter around it and serve hot.

CRUISSES DES GRENOUILLES POULETTE
(Frog Legs Poulette)

Put your frog legs well seasoned with salt and white pepper in a sauce pan with a good deal of butter and saute same; when done drain off, replace frog legs in saucepan and add a sauce poulette made of chicken stock well thickened; add stock of frog legs. If too light, reduce same and add chopped fine herbs before serving in a chafing dish; also sprinkle fine chopped slices of mushrooms.

CHICKEN A LA KING

Take according to number of persons the quantity of boiled young chicken, the supremes and fillets mignons of the breasts and chop same; put them in a sauce pan with a piece of butter and salt and let get warm, add enough double cream to cover the meat and cook slowly for ten or fifteen minutes and finish off, thickening with a piece of fresh butter, steadily stirring; add little cayenne, peeled

Their Chafing Dish Specialties

chopped green peppers and diced mushrooms which have been cooked in butter; mix well and serve in chafing dish and garnish with slices of very black truffles.

EMINCEE DE RIZ DE VEAU FINANCIER
(Emincee of Sweetbreads Financiere)

Take a small sweetbread for each person, boil in salt water or braize same with onions, carrots, whole peppers, fine herbs, for twenty minutes. Let cool off; take its stock and add a little tomato sauce, some demiglaze and let cook a few minutes. Strain and put in casserole place same on stove; taste if well seasoned then add your sweetbreads, cut in dice and mix whole well while adding mushrooms, truffles, coxcombs, chicken quenelles and a little madeira and serve hot in chafing dish.

Emile Bailly

G. R. MEYER
CHEF
RECTOR'S
Chicago, Ill.
With finest hotels in Europe, also the Auditorium, Congress and College Inn, Chicago.

CHICKEN LYDIA

Take the breast of a nice chicken which has previously been boiled in a good spiced chicken stock. Cut in julienne (shreds) ten ounces of breast, three ounces of fresh mushrooms, washed, cooked and shredded like the chicken, one green pepper washed and cleaned of its seeds, cut in fine shreds and smother in butter without obtaining color. Put all these ingredients in a sauce pan, moisten with a little fresh mushroom and chicken stock and heat all together. Then pour to their height with sauce supreme and boil for about three minutes, season to taste, dress in chafing dish, garnish the top with a small tender heart or bottom of an artichoke previously heated in butter and serve hot.

 # WORLD FAMOUS CHEFS

SAUCE SUPREME

Put four gills of clear poultry stock and one gill of mushroom liquid into a sauce pan, reduce to two-thirds of original amount, then add two gills of chicken veloute, reduce on the open fire, stirring with a wooden spoon constantly, add gradually four gills of good cream, season to taste and strain through a sieve when light and succulent.

For fresh mushroom stock, peel and wash the mushrooms, put in a sauce pan, cover to its height with chicken stock, a little good butter and a little lemon juice, boil slowly for about five minutes.

Chicken Veloute is made from good strong and clear chicken stock, well spiced. Take a sauce pan, place some good butter in it, when hot but white, add flour as much as to absorb the butter, let simmer for a while, stirring often, being careful not to let it brown, then add chicken stock, slowly until it is a thin liquid. Let boil for about twenty minutes or longer if necessary until a light sauce is obtained; skim occasionally as it boils. Season with salt and pepper and a little nutmeg, strain through a sieve into a bowl and use when needed.

LOBSTER NEWBERG

Take two live lobsters weighing about two pounds each; boil in salt water with a few spices for about twenty minutes. When cold detach the bodies from the tail and cut the latter into slices; put them into a sauce pan and add a little hot butter; season well with salt and pepper and fry lightly on both sides; moisten with a half gill madeira wine and reduce sauce to half of its original amount. Then moisten to their height with good cream and boil down to three quarters of the full amount, after which thicken with a previously made thickening, of four tablespoonfuls of raw cream, one tablespoonful of madeira wine, two yolks of eggs, a pinch of cayenne; incorporate with lobster, add a little butter, cook without boiling, tossing the lobster lightly, then put in a chafing dish and serve quickly.

LOBSTER ABINITIO

Take the meat from two live lobsters, season with salt and pepper; put in a sauce pan a little butter and sweet oil. When hot put the lobster into it and fry on both sides lightly; add some chopped shallots

THEIR CHAFING DISH SPECIALTIES

and a few slices of fresh mushrooms; then add two gills of brandy and five gills of white wine, two gills of brown madeira sauce, one ripe tomato, peeled and chopped finely; a little thyme; cover the sauce pan and cook for about ten minutes. Add then the creamy parts of the lobster together with a piece of butter and the juice of a lemon, a little chopped parsley. Heat well together without boiling, season, put in a chafing dish and serve hot.

CRAB MEAT NORFOLK

Cut one small onion and one green pepper in small juliennes, also a few fresh mushrooms sliced. Put a little oil in a sauce pan and fry the onion, pepper and mushrooms for about eight minutes together without coloring; add two fresh tomatoes peeled and cut in small pieces; cook together for about five minutes, moisten with two gills of white wine and let simmer for about five minutes more. Add one pint of crab meat, season to taste and add a clove of crushed garlic. Mix all well together with one-half gill of tomato sauce and when it starts to boil, put in a chafing dish and serve hot.

G. R. Meyer.

 # WORLD FAMOUS CHEFS

VICTOR HIRTZLER
CHEF DE CUISINE
HOTEL
ST. FRANCIS
San Francisco, Cal.

Mr. Hirtzler was born in Strasbourg, Alsace, Germany, and learned his profession under Emile Feypell in Strasbourg who is considered one of the finest Chefs in France. Mr. Hirtzler has been in the best hotels in France and Germany. Coming to the United States he started in at the Old Brunswick in New York City, and then at the Waldorf Astoria, New York City, then at Sherry's famous Cafe, New York City. He came to San Francisco to open the Hotel St. Francis in 1904.

SWEET BREADS MONZA

Having parboiled the sweetbreads, rinse in cold water, then slice into pieces a quarter of an inch thick, of the size of half a dollar. Put into saute pan with two ounces of butter, salt and pepper, and simmer for five minutes. At the same time, take another saute pan into which put two ounces of butter with a dozen fresh mushrooms which have been sliced thin, and after simmering in the butter for ten minutes, drain this butter, which is too brown to use, and add the drained mushrooms to the sweetbreads. Add half a pint of cream. Let come to boiling point. Mix two yolks with a cup of cream and add this, letting it heat until creamy, but do not boil.

FONDUE SAVARIN

Fondue is a mixture of cheese, eggs, cream made into a light, creamy consistency as follows. Place the yolks of eight eggs in a pan with half a pound of butter broken into bits and eight ounces of grated cheese; season with cayenne, salt and a little black pepper. Put on the fire in a double boiler, whisking with a wire spoon until it thickens. Serve on toasted bread.

FINNAN HADDIE IN CREAM

Procure the tiny patty shapes at the baker's and fill. Parboil the smoked fish, then pick it to bits, discarding the bones and skin. Heat a little milk and cream, thicken with cornstarch, then add the fish adding salt and pepper. This is a savory dish.

CREAMED FINNAN HADDIE

Parboil the smoked fish. Remove from the bones and skin. Put into saucepan with a cup of cream. Simmer slowly, thickening

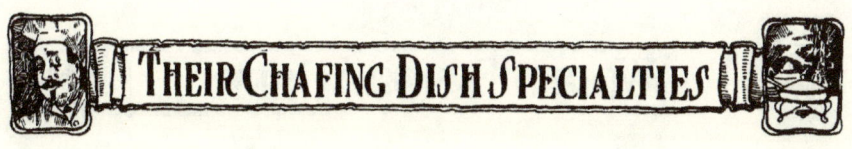

Their Chafing Dish Specialties

with moistened cornstarch. When ready to serve, add pepper. Serve on toast.

CRAB MEAT IN CREAM

Take one boiled crab, taken out of shell (called crab meat). Put in saucepan a piece of butter size of an egg, let it get warm, add two soupspoonsful of sifted flour, let get hot; when hot, add one pint of boiling milk and one-fourth of a pint hot cream. Stir well and boil for ten minutes. Salt and cayenne pepper, then add the crab meat and serve in deep dish. Dry toast to be served with it.

CRAB MEAT MONZA

One pound of fresh mushrooms nicely washed, cut each mushroom in four, put in saucepan with two ounces of butter, let simmer for a half-hour. When mushrooms are soft, add crab meat in cream of one crab. Before serving, pour in one whisky glassful of best dry sherry wine.

CRAB MEAT GOURMET

One-fourth of a pound of pickled shrimps put in a saucepan. Add one ounce of butter and one-half whisky glassful of dry sherry wine; let simmer for five minutes, then add the crab meat monza of one crab.

TERRAPIN MARYLAND

Put one cup of terrapin, prepared as below, in flat pan. Add a little grated nutmeg, salt and pepper and half a glass of dry sherry. Boil till half reduced, then add a cup of thick cream, boil, and thicken with yolks of two eggs mixed and beaten with a quarter cup of thick cream and one ounce of butter. Heat, but do not boil this. Serve in chafing dish, with dry sherry and toast on the side.

How to Boil Terrapin

Take two live terrapin and put into boiling water for two minutes. Remove from water. With a towel remove the outer skin from feet, neck and head. Then put terrapin in kettle with two quarts of cold water, an onion, a carrot, a bay leaf, one clove, boiling until feet are

WORLD FAMOUS CHEFS

soft. The time depends upon the age of the terrapin, some being cooked in fifteen minutes, and others requiring two or three hours. When done, open the shell, take out all the meat, including the liver, from which remove the gall with scissors. Remove tail and claws and head. Cut the legs in inch-long pieces or at the joints, as preferred. Put all in jar, having first reduced the broth by boiling it down, the remaining quantity being about a cupful. Add a whisky glass of sherry wine. Leave meat in this broth. Then prepare the terrapin in any style desired.

TERRAPIN JOCKEY CLUB

Same as above. Before serving, add two ponies of cognac and six slices of truffles.

TERRAPIN BALTIMORE

On cup of terrapin without the liver. Put into saucepan with salt, pepper, nutmeg, celery salt, a glass of dry sherry and boil for five minutes. Now mash the liver in a salad bowl, adding two raw yolks, one ounce of sweet butter, straining through fine sieve. Now add a cup of brown sauce to the simmering terrapin, then add the liver prepared as above, pouring in gradually. Barely heat this enough to thicken. Before serving add half a glass of dry sherry.

OYSTERS OR CRAB A LA POULETTE

If for oysters prepare by boiling them in their own liquid for about five minutes. If the small California oysters are used boil for half that time. Into this liquid—say a pint of oysters—stir a heaping teaspoonful of cornstarch which has been moistened with half a pint of white wine. Beat the yolks of two eggs with half a cup of cream and stir slowly into the above. Add two large spoonsful of butter. Do not let come to a boil. Squeeze into this the juice of half a small lemon. If making the sauce for crab have the crab cut into small pieces. Make the sauce just the same, except in place of beginning with the broth of the oyster for the foundation of the sauce begin with a cup and a half of cream and water in equal proportions. Then thicken with cornstarch, add the yolks and so on just the same, putting the crab meat in last.

Their Chafing Dish Specialties

CURRIED CRAB

Cut the crab meat into small pieces. Take butter the size of an egg, add a teaspoonful of chopped onion or shallot. Fry to a golden brown. Add a heaping teaspoonful of flour and a small teaspoonful of curry powder, stirring into the butter and onion until thoroughly mixed. Add a cup of hot soup stock and a cup of cream. Boil for three minutes. Add the crab meat and simmer slowly for about five minutes. Serve with boiled rice.

SHRIMP WITH MUSHROOMS

Fry two cups of shrimps in plenty of butter, allowing half a cup of chopped mushrooms. Add some nutmeg, seasoning and the juice of half a lemon. Add two spoonsful of tomato sauce and half a cup of stock and a few bread crumbs. Sprinkle with parsley.

CRAB IN CHAFING DISH

Mince an onion, preferably a shallot onion, browning slightly with two spoonsful of butter. Add a spoonful of flour, mixing well. Then add a half pint of sweet milk. Stir to a smooth cream. Add the meat of a small crab and a tablespoonful of sherry. Pour over toast cut in fancy shapes, serving on a deep platter.

FROGS A LA POULETTE

Cut the legs in two at the joint. To a pound of legs, allow six ounces of fresh minced mushrooms. Fry in butter with the mushrooms, adding half a pint of veloute sauce when fried—this being a highly seasoned soup stock—and after simmering for a few minutes, thicken with three raw egg yolks mixed with a half cup of cream. Season with salt, cayenne, nutmeg, chopped parsley and the juice of half a lemon. It should be served hot, preferably in a chafing dish.

SLICED FILLET OF BEEF A LA ESTRAGON

Slice lean fillet of beef size of a silver dollar; put in hot butter in chafing dish. Add two chopped shallots, cook quickly on good fire for three minutes then add chopped estragon, a fresh piece of butter and the juice of a lemon. Serve.

 # WORLD FAMOUS CHEFS

EGGS BECHAMEL
Six hard boiled eggs cut in two. Put some cream in chafing dish, when hot thicken with a little cornstarch, add salt, pepper and the eggs, also chives if desired.

FINNAN HADDIE
Skin one forman haddock cut in small pieces. Put in chafing dish with one-half pint of cream, let cook for twenty minutes then mix two yolks of eggs with a little cream and thicken the fish and serve. Do not let it boil with the egg in it.

FROGLEGS MICHELS
Take the legs of twelve frogs, put in chafing dish with a piece of butter, salt and pepper. Let simmer for three minutes then add one chopped shallot and simmer for two minutes. Then add a pony of white wine, cook for two minutes; one-half cup of cream sauce and one-half cup of tomato sauce, chopped parsley and let simmer for five minutes. Just before dishing out add a good piece of sweet butter.

Their Chafing Dish Specialties

JOHN PFAFF
CHEF DE CUISINE
HOTEL CAPE MAY
Cape May, N. J.

Mr. John Pfaff has been at the following hotels: Hotel Marie Antoinette, New York City, Hotel Metropole, Philadelphia, Brighton Beach, at Coney Island, New York; the Hotel Kaaterskill, Kaaterskill, N. Y

CHICKEN A LA KING

Mince the white meat of two breasts of chicken; slice eight fresh mushrooms and stew in two ounces of butter. Take a pint of cream and put chicken and mushrooms in pan and add one gill of sherry and two more ounces of butter. Mix well and as soon as it starts to boil put in chafing dish. Slice one whole truffle thin and lay across the top. Serve with thin dry toast on hot plates.

CRAB FLAKES, NEWBERG

Take one pint of crab flakes and put in two ounces of melted butter. Add one gill of sherry. Put on fire for two or three minutes or until it gets hot. Add one pint of good cream and let cook for one minute. Take off fire and add the yolks of three eggs. Stir thoroughly. Add two ounces more of butter and another gill of sherry. Keep on stirring and put in chafing dish. Do not let it boil at any time. Serve with hot toast on the side.

SWEETBREAD A LA HOTEL CHAMPLAIN

Take four nice calf's sweetbreads and plunge well. After they are cold, slice in pieces and saute in butter for six minutes. Also have eight fresh mushrooms sauted in butter for six minutes. Put mushrooms and sweetbreads in sauce pan in which a pint of good cream has been placed and add one ounce of butter. Add one sliced pimento and stir thoroughly for three minutes. Add one gill of sherry while stirring. Stir until it simmers. Slice some truffles and lay in sherry until ready to serve. When ready, put mixture in chafing dish and spread the truffles all over the top. Season to taste.

John Pfaff.

WORLD FAMOUS CHEFS

JOSEPH STOLTZ
CHEF DE CUISINE
HOTEL
PONCE DE LEON
St. Augustine, Fla.

Mr. Stoltz was formerly at the National Arts Club, New York City; later with the Metropole Hotel, New York City and the Country Club, Detroit, Mich.

FROG LEGS

First select eighteen pair of good sized frog's legs. Take clean off the bone; add twelve fresh mushrooms peeled, blanched and cut in small squares. Saute all these together in two ounces of fresh butter. Five minutes afterwards add one demitasse of good sherry wine. Now put this aside and cover. Five minutes later, add one-half pint of medium thick cream, dilute tablespoonful of arrowroot and thicken; then add eighteen medium oysters that have been blanched and from which the tough part has been removed. Season the whole to taste, not forgetting to use paprika which gives the snappy taste. Put in chafing dish and place six soft poached eggs all around in line on top of contents. Serve while very hot and finish with a couple dozen toast sippetts. This is sufficient for six people.

SWEETBREADS

Blanch six nice sweetbreads, trim and lard with smoked beef tongue and truffles. Place in pan, a little vegetable and braise to a light brown color. Cut up six shallots and one good sized green pepper peeled and cut in small squares. Saute together with two ounces of fresh butter. In about five minutes add one demitasse full of good sherry and one pint of sweet cream, heat contents on side of stove, slowly; now dilute two tablespoonfuls of rice flour and thicken, let come to boiling point slowly; keep shaking sauce while cooking to prevent it from catching to bottom. Now add two ounces more of fresh butter and one-half demitasse of sherry; have two dozen parisienne potatoes boiled, place these in sauce. Then place sweetbreads in the chafing dish on a nice round piece of toast. Pour the sauce gently over sweetbreads, leave a round space in the middle of chafing dish and place there one large cup of freshly cooked new green peas. Place the parisienne potatoes all around the edge of the

Their Chafing Dish Specialties

sweetbreads. Sprinkle each sweetbread with a light dash of paprika. Cover and serve while very hot.

SQUAB CHICKEN

Take three nice plump full breasted squab chickens, lift the breast clean from the bones, prepare as for a supreme only omitting the force meat. Put these six fillets or supremes in a buttered pan and cover with very thin slices of salt pork. Braise them for about twenty minutes in a medium hot oven. If the oven is too hot cover with paper. Baste with chicken stock while cooking, keeping them moist and preventing them from becoming hard. They must not be allowed to become brown or dry. When this is done, place them on the side for further use. Chop fine, one onion, saute in two ounces of fresh butter not letting it turn brown; add to this two red peppers cut in small squares, one cupful of mushrooms cut into quarters, then one cupful of good white wine. Let simmer a few minutes, then add one pint of sauce allemande, which sauce consists of three ounces of fresh butter, four tablespoonfuls of flour and one pint of chicken broth or stock, three yolks of raw eggs and the juice of one-fourth lemon, season to taste. Now place supremes of chicken each one on top of a very hot artichoke bottom. Leave a hollow in center of chafing dish, pour garnish of chicken and in center opening place a nice bouquet of asparagus tips, being careful to stand them erect, then besprinkle each fillet with very finely chopped truffles. Serve this while very hot. This is sufficient for six people.

Joseph Stoltz

WORLD FAMOUS CHEFS

MARTIN GINDER
CHEF DE CUISINE
HOTEL GREEN
Pasadena, Cal.

Mr. Ginder was apprenticed in France in the best hotels. He was at the New York Athletic Club, the Princeton Club, the old Hotel Metropole, Cafe Savarin and the Vendome Hotel, New York City. He has also held several important positions in the middle west prior to taking his present position.

SHAD ROE SAUTE

Boil two fresh roe about ten minutes in chafing dish in salt water. Then remove it and let get very cold. Cut them in half pieces and set in well buttered chafing dish and fry them slowly on both sides. Finish them as lobster saute.

SCRAMBLED EGGS

Cut about a cupful of bread in small dice; fry it in chafing dish in butter until brown, not too brown. Add six fresh eggs and scramble them soft or hard as you desire. Season with salt and pepper; also small dice of ham or bacon can be fried with the bread.

OYSTER CREAM SAUCE

Let four dozen large open oysters boil in their own juice about two minutes. As soon as they get firm, drain them, season with salt, cayenne pepper and nutmeg. Put two tablespoonsful of melted butter in your chafing dish and a tablespoonful of flour; let this mix well on a slow fire, then add hot cream or milk until it makes a thick cream sauce. Let this boil about five minutes and when ready to serve add the oysters and stir in a piece of good butter. Serve on toast with chopped parsley. A little sherry wine may be added if desired.

WELSH RAREBIT GOURMANT

Cut some best quality American cheese, old and yellow is the best, in firm small pieces. Put this into chafing dish. One pound of cheese should be enough for four people. One gill of beer (ale) a pinch of red pepper and a small pinch of dry mustard. Stir the mixture with a small wire whisk on a full blaze in your chafing dish until the cheese is melted and flowing. Lay on a hot serving dish, two slices of toasted bread. Before pouring the melted cheese on

the toast add a teaspoonful of yellow cornmeal, mix in slowly and serve hot.

MINCED CHICKEN A LA GREEN

Cut up a breast of boiled fowl in half inch slices. Fry a little chopped onion, chop a red pepper, one green pepper, pimento and six fresh mushrooms on hot fire in chafing dish without coloring. Finish the same as lobsters and serve on hot toast. To keep the remainder hot, set the pan in your water dish.

LOBSTER

Cook two lobsters weighing about two pounds in boiling water for about twenty-five minutes. When cold, detach the bodies from the tails and cut the latter into slices. Put them into a chafing dish on the full fire easily, lying flat, and add a hot piece of clarified butter, season with salt and a little paprika and a little ground nutmeg. Fry lightly on both sides without coloring, moisten to their height with good cream. Reduce quickly to half and then add two or three teaspoonfuls of Madeira wine, boil the liquid about two minutes, then remove and thicken with a thickening of four egg yolks mixed with a little cream. Cook without boiling, stirring constantly until it thickens; remove from fire and serve on hot toast.

WORLD FAMOUS CHEFS

HENRY JOHANNSEN
CHEF DE CUISINE
HOTEL
ROYAL PALM
Miami, Fla.

Mr. Johannsen was at the Country Club, Brooklyn, Mass., Maplewood Hotel, White Mountains, N. H., Hotel Alcazar, St. Augustine, Fla., and at the Oriental Hotel, Manhattan Beach, N. Y.

LOBSTER, ARISTOCRAT

Devil one large lobster, broil same till done; take out the meat, place in chafing dish. Add one-half teaspoonful of fresh chives, two to three tablespoonfuls of butter, let simmer for a few minutes, then serve with dry toast separate.

CAPON, BIGARURE

One-half breast of capon, one-half veal sweetbread, one-half lamb fries cooked and cut in one-half inch pieces; saute separate, six to eight fresh mushrooms with a little shallots or chives. Place altogether in a sauce pan and add one glass of good wine, and season to taste. Let simmer for a few minutes then add a glass of extra heavy cream. Let simmer for about five minutes more, finish with the yolk of two eggs and a lump of best butter before serving.

MELI, "MELO" ROYAL PALACE

Two small Norwegian fish cakes, six slices Finnan Haddie sliced, four pieces Tuna fish, cut in about three-fourths or one inch pieces, six large soft clam (only the heart), six to eight large fresh shrimps. Saute one small shallot and one or two green peppers cut in small pieces about one-fourth of an inch in good butter to a golden brown color. Add one glass of sherry wine, one glass of heavy cream so as to cover the whole. Place all together in a saucepan, let simmer for about five to eight minutes. Finish with a lump of good sweet butter.

Henry Johannsen

Their Chafing Dish Specialties

CHAS. A. FREY
CHEF
HOTEL ALEXANDRIA
Los Angeles, Cal.

Mr. Frey was first at the Hotel von Konig von England in Munster; later at the Dom Hotel, Cologne; Continental Hotel, Paris; with the North German Lloyd and Hamburg-American Steamship Lines and Hotel Bellevue-Stratford, Philadelphia.

CRAB A LA CLEOPATRE

Boil two gallons of water, season with four half lemons, two onions, a small bunch of parsley, about five ounces of salt, two ounces whole black pepper. Place two hard shell crabs in the liquid, let boil for twenty minutes and let get cold in same.

Remove the meat off body and legs so same will not be badly broken up. Place in saucepan, one-fourth pound butter, saute the crab meat and also three pimentoes roasted, peeled and cut in strips one-half inch long, also three-fourths pound cepes, salt and pepper (cayenne) to suit, add one-half pint sherry wine, let braize for five minutes, add one quart of boiling cream and shortly after a thickening of ten yolks of eggs three ounces of butter and one-fourth pint of double cream. Thoroughly mix the contents of your sauce pan with the thickening, let come to a boil, and serve immediately in chafing dish on toast.

SLICES OF CAPON FORESTIERE

Clean a seven pound capon, place in saucepan with two chopped carrots, two celery, two onions and small bunch of parsley, salt, whole pepper, a few bay leaves and one-fourth pound of butter. Cover the capon with salt pork, slowly braise the capon and from time to time add a little chicken broth. When cooked remove skin and slice the breast.

Have in a saucepan six ounces of melted butter, saute one pound sliced morilles and six sliced artichoke bottoms and slices of capon. Add a thickening of twelve yolks of eggs, four ounces butter, one-fourth pint double cream.. Pour the thickening in saucepan and thoroughly mix the contents with the thickening and a glass of Madeira wine. Let come to boil. Serve immediately in chafing dish with cheese sticks if preferred.

Charles A. Frey

WORLD FAMOUS CHEFS

FANCY AND CHAFING DISHES FOR PARTIES AND HOTEL VIRGINIA SPECIAL DISHES

WILLIAM LEON BENZENI
CHEF DE CUISINE
HOTEL VIRGINIA
Long Beach, Cal.

Mr. Benzeni learned his trade at the Hotel Metropole in Geneva, Switzerland. Afterward he was employed at Stutgart, Wurtemberg, Germany. He was connected with several prominent hotels in the East prior to coming west to take the position at the Hotel Virginia.

PLANKED CROWN OF MILK LAMB

Have a round plank with deep border about twelve by twelve around; place a full crown of lamb on the plank; blanch in the oven for about five or six minutes, then garnish crown of lamb with beechnut bacon and a fancy border of duchess potatoes around, put back in the oven just six minutes before serving. Have some French flageolet with fresh butter and chopped parsley; pour in the middle of the crown on the plank, garnish with fresh mint and serve hot.

REED BIRD A LA PAUL LECOURT

Have a dozen nice fat reed birds; put a basting spoonful of olive oil in a sauce pan, place on the range and when hot put your reed bird in and a good handful of bay seeds; season with salt and pepper, toss on a good fire for ten minutes; when good and brown add the juice of two lemons. Serve at once in a hot chafing dish with some thin toast. A very dainty after-theatre party dish.

FILET OF STRIPED BASS A LA C. STANLEY

Place twelve rolled and seasoned filet of striped bass in a santoir with fresh butter, cover and let cook three minutes; add a half dozen chopped green onions. Cook two minutes more then cover the fish with a pint of Rhine wine, a cupful of river shrimp, three sliced truffles and a dozen oysters; let cook all of ten minutes. Then make a roux and pour the juice of the fish in it, add the yolks of three eggs, juice of a lemon and a pinch of paprika. Place the fish in a chafing dish with all the garnish, strain the sauce through a small sieve and serve hot with graham toast.

THEIR CHAFING DISH SPECIALTIES

TOMATO FRICASSEE IN A CHAFING DISH

Peel a dozen small, ripe tomatoes, season with salt and pepper, roll or dust with flour, fry in a saucepan with clarified butter; place in a chafing dish and cover with a cupful of best cream, a teaspoonful of sugar and a dash of cayenne. Toss on the fire for five minutes. If you are careful you will have a dainty dish for lunch. Serve saltine wafers with it.

FLANKED SHAD DINNER A LA MAYOR STOY

Have a large fish plank, prepare a fresh shad and blanched roe, oil and place in a hot oven for ten minutes, take out and arrange a fine border of duchess potatoes, put back in the oven just ten minutes before serving. Garnish on one end with fresh peas and the other end with small Parisienne potatoes. Place the roe in the middle and eight to ten soft shell crabs fried crisp. Arrange some scalloped radishes around, black and green olives and fancy cut lemon, and branch of parsley. Finish with a hot nut brown butter.

LOBSTER A LA AMERICAINE

Select a large fresh lobster, take out of the shell and cut up in large dice, place in saucepan on the range with a large glass of best brandy. Toss until brandy is almost all burned and reduced, add a large piece of good butter, salt and paprika, a pint of tomatoes, one-half pint of button mushrooms and cook for ten minutes. Add a dash of cayenne pepper and serve hot with browned croutons in chafing dish.

SPAGHETTI FOR LUNCHEON

Put a package of spaghetti in a gallon of boiling water with a handful of salt; cook about eighteen to twenty minutes according to the brand. Place a small pot on the range with a spoonful of clarified butter, drop in a clove of chopped garlic, half an onion and a piece of ham trimming; when brown put in one quart of tomatoes, salt and pepper and a bay leaf; reduce to one-half; drain the spaghetti and strain the tomato sauce over and add a piece of table butter the size of a walnut, and a pinch of nutmeg. Serve hot in a chafing dish with

WORLD FAMOUS CHEFS

grated Parmesan cheese on the side. An addition of shredded smoked tongue, button mushrooms and rings of stoned olives make a variety, good for a change.

ROAST SQUAB CHICKEN A LA LENA FRANK

Prepare one or two dry-picked squab chickens, cut the neck in the back and with your thumb lift the skin from the breast which will form a pocket. Make a dressing with fine chopped salt pork, green onions, fresh thyme, parsley, salt and pepper and white bread crumbs, add one egg and do not make too moist. Place this dressing over the breast and under the skin and also inside the chicken; cover with a slice of salt pork. Cut wide and thin so as to cover the whole breast. Now put the chicken in a casserole and place small carrots and turnips and button onion around it, cover with clarified butter and cook twenty to twenty-five minutes in a medium hot oven. Take the trusses from the chicken; place the vegetables around it with a few sprigs of fresh parsley and serve in a covered dish.

Their Chafing Dish Specialties

E. C. PERAULT
CHEF DE CUISINE
PLANTERS HOTEL
St. Louis, Mo.

Mr. Perault was born in Lyon, France. On coming to this country was at the Mercantile and University Clubs, St. Louis, Grand Hotel Mackinac, Mackinac, Mich.; the Eastman Hotel, Hot Springs; and the Antlers, Colorado Springs.

CHICKEN SPECIAL

Take the breast of a boiled hen scalloped very thin and boiled Virginia ham, also scalloped very thin; put in chafing dish with cream; when it comes to a boil, add a little tomato sauce; mix in a little flour with drawn butter, keep stirring until it becomes a little thick; season with paprika, nutmeg and salt; when ready put in very fine cut chives and serve with toast and steamed dry rice.

SEA FOODS—CHAFING DISH

Take scalloped oysters, boiled lobster, fresh crab chunks or fresh shrimp, put a lump of butter in chafing dish with sliced fresh mushrooms, add a little sherry wine; let simmer down until mushrooms are done, then put in the shell fish. Put the yolks of three eggs in a bowl with one and one-half pints cream, season with nutmeg, paprika, salt, then mix well and pour same in the chafing dish, keep shaking slowly until it becomes thick, add a little sherry wine and butter and serve with toast or toasted English muffins.

SWEETBREADS A LA PLANTERS

Take two pair raw sweetbreads, blanch them and when cold slice very thin; put in chafing dish with a little Madeira wine, let simmer slowly, add cream. When boiling, add a little flour with drawn butter until it becomes thick, season with nutmeg, pepper, salt and put in two fine chopped hard boiled eggs, and a little chopped chives, then add a little Madeira wine and a little butter. Serve with toast on side or with patties; can also be added with mushroom morrels or cepes.

Edmond Perault

WORLD FAMOUS CHEFS

CHAFING DISH SPECIALTIES

JULES DAUVILLER
CHEF DE CUISINE
PALACE HOTEL
San Francisco, Cal.

Mr. Dauviller was formerly the $10,000 a year dictator of the cuisine in the home of Mr. and Mrs. Harry Payne Whitney in New York. The Whitneys got him from the Grand Hotel in Paris. He served his apprenticeship in the Cafe de la Paix at Marguery and the Hotel Chabot at the French Capital, before taking responsible positions with the Hotel Riveria at Nice, Italy and the Grand Hotel at Paris. He succeeded to the position of Chef at the Palace in San Francisco upon the resignation of Mr. Ernest Arbogast.

SCRAMBLED EGGS MAJOR RATHBONE
(For six persons)

Two medium green bell peppers cut in dices, also four tomatoes, cut same way, place a piece of butter the size of an egg in your chafing dish and start to heat up; when warm add your green peppers and let simmer for a few minutes, then add tomatoes, stir the whole continuously. Take one dozen fresh eggs well beaten and seasoned. Add all the rest in chafing dish and in the last moment add either three dozen half cooked (in butter) California oysters or one dozen eastern oysters, and serve on slices of toast.

RISDE VEAU PALACE

Calf Sweetbreads Palace (For six persons)

Choose six calf sweetbreads cooked, while on the other hand take three dozen small white mushrooms, two green peppers and two pimentoes cut in julien. Place and melt in your chafing dish three ounces butter; when hot put your mushrooms in it and cook for a few minutes, then add sweetbreads which have been seasoned. Cover your chafing dish and let cook for fifteen minutes, add then your green peppers and pimentoes, and one pint of thick cream; let the whole cook for a few minutes and add a little sherry amontillado and serve on waffles.

CRAB FLAKES A LA KING
(For six persons)

One and one-half pounds of crab flakes, two green peppers cut in dices, butter size of an egg place in chafing dish; when hot put your peppers in it and cook for a few minutes, gradually add crab flakes.

Their Chafing Dish Specialties

Season well with salt, paprika and muscat; mix the whole well and add one pint of thick cream let boil few minutes and add little Oloroso sherry before serving. Serve on toast with a few slices of truffles.

FROG LEGS CHINJARADA
(For six persons)

Twelve well cleaned frog saddles, chop green onions very fine, take three ounces of butter, heat in your chafing dish; when hot put frog legs with little garlic (chopped fine) in it, stir and cover few minutes; when cooked add your chopped onions; on the other hand have a bowl with six yolks of eggs, spoonful of water, same of white wine vinegar, pour over frog legs and stir continuously and serve hot.

J. Danviller

WORLD FAMOUS CHEFS

LOUIS LESCARBOURA
CHEF DE CUISINE
FT. PITT HOTEL
Pittsburg, Pa.

Prior to coming to the Fort Pitt Hotel, Mr. Lescarboura was Chef at the Hotel Marlborough, New York City, and other prominent eastern hotels, and was Entremetier at the famous "Delmonico's Cafe," New York City.

CRAB FLAKES SUBLIME

One pint of crab flakes, six sliced fresh mushrooms, six slices of Virginia ham, two egg yolks, two tablespoons of sherry. Fry the mushrooms and ham in chafing dish till brown and add the crab flakes, pour in cream, season with salt and cayenne pepper; let boil for ten minutes; beat the yolks with the sherry and with it thicken the preparation. Lay the slices of ham on six slices of toast, divide the crab meat over same and serve.

CHAFING DISH PEPITA

Meat of a boiled fowl, six fresh mushrooms, one red pepper, three peeled tomatoes, one small glass white wine, six chopped shallots, one cup tomato sauce. Cut the boiled fowl in squares. Cook the mushrooms till lightly browned, add the shallots, stir well; add the wine, let it reduce to half; add the tomatoes and cook till melted; add the pimento, chicken and tomato sauce. Season with pepper. Mix well, cover the dish and cook very slowly for twenty minutes. Serve boiled rice with it.

CHAFING DISH KNICKERBOCKER

Meat of a large boiled lobster cut in squares, three cooked calf sweetbreads, one green pepper, six fresh mushrooms, one pint cream two egg yolks, one ounce pecans, one ounce good butter. Heat a piece of good butter in chafing dish add the pepper and mushrooms, fry till lightly brown; add the lobster and sweetbreads, season with salt and paprika, and a little curry powder, pour in a tablespoonful of brandy and one of sherry, light it and when the flame goes out add the cream, mix well and let boil for ten minutes. Thicken the preparation with the yolks. Remove the dish from the fire and add little by little the butter. Serve toast separate.

Louis Lescarboura

Their Chafing Dish Specialties

HENRI D. FOUILLOUX
CHEF-STEWARD
ST. CHARLES HOTEL
New Orleans, La.

Mr. Fouilloux served his apprenticeship at the Maison Arwaud of Paris, France. Was later at the Hotel du Rhin, Paris, with Baron de Neaflize at Paris, with Mr. Vayne McVeah — American Ambassador in Rome, with Count Moroni Pecci at Rome, Leo XIII at the Vatican in Rome, Madame Melba in London, for Viscount Bulkeley at Beaumaris in North Wales and at the Grand Hotel in Rome. Coming to this country, he was at the Hollenden Hotel, Cleveland.

IMPERIAL STEW

Place in a pan called (Plat a saute) the meat of a medium sized cold boiled lobster cut in medium size dice, eight or ten New York counts oysters, one calf brain cut same size, one large white braized sweetbread; cut also one dozen large shrimps, eight or ten medium size peeled fresh mushrooms, four or five spoonsful of hot butter, a pony of brandy, seasoning with salt, pepper, paprika a dash of cayenne pepper and put same on very hot fire for one or two minutes, add a full pint of rich cream, let boil few minutes; mix five yolks of eggs with a glass of cream and slowly mix same till soon you notice the Newburg thickening; take off from the fire, add a good glass of sherry wine and serve immediately on your chafing dish with toast on the side.

BREAST OF MALLARD DUCK AU PORTO

Take a large mallard duck, dress same for roasting, not stuffed; cook same very rare about twelve minutes on very hot oven; cut the breast of filets of each side and cut those on the long way about one-half inch thick; place these on a chafing dish. Take your duck carcass (bones) chop same and press on regular duck press, take this juice, add two spoonsful of currant jelly and two ounces of good port wine, pour same on top of your duck breast seasoning with salt and paprika. Take your chafing dish in the dining room and finish cooking, serve with slices of oranges.

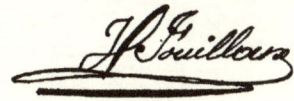

WORLD FAMOUS CHEFS

LOUIS PFAFF
CHEF DE CUISINE
NEW WILLARD HOTEL
Washington, D. C.

Mr. Pfaff was formerly at the following prominent New York City hotels. The St. Denis, The Union Square, The Albemarle, The Vendome, The New Amsterdam; also at the Royal Moskoko at Ontario, Canada.

LOBSTER, MEXICAINE

Boil three lobsters, take out meat from tail and cut into pieces half inch thick, saute in pan with butter; add tomatoes, rice, red peppers; simmer about ten minutes; serve in chafing dish, after seasoning to taste. Quantity sufficient for three persons.

TERRAPIN (Stewed)

Put on terrapin in boiling water for two minutes, remove the outer skin, then boil in water with spices until well done; cut meat into small pieces. Stir in pan with butter, salt pepper and sherry; serve in chafing dish. Quantity sufficient for two persons.

CHICKEN A LA KING

Boil one fowl until well done, cut up breast meat into small cubes; quarter pound fresh mushrooms and saute with butter, then add chicken and a pint of cream; boil for five minutes, and add tablespoon bechamel sauce, salt, and paprika. Serve in chafing dish. Quantity sufficient for three persons.

CRAB FLAKES A LA DEWEY

Take one pound flakes, half pound fresh mushrooms, a few oyster crabs, half a green pepper; saute the mushrooms and pepper in a little butter, add pint of cream and flakes and stew for five minutes, season to taste, serve in chafing dish. Quantity sufficient for four persons.

Louis Pfaff

Their Chafing Dish Specialties

EMILE BURGERMEISTER
CHEF DE CUISINE
HOTEL FAIRMONT
San Francisco, Cal.

Mr. Burgermeister was assistant to Mr. Emile Bailly, the well known Chef of the St. Regis, New York City, and worked with him at the Grand Hotel at Monte Carlo, France; at the Hotel Adlon, Berlin, Germany; the Frankfurter-hof, at Frankfurt, Germany, and the Pavilion Royal at Paris. He worked under Wm. A. Escoffier at the famous Ritz-Carlton Hotel in London, to learn the wonderful Ritz-Carlton organization.

CRAB FLAKES MADRAS

Mince a small onion, brown lightly in butter, mince one green apple, mix one teaspoonful of curry powder, a little powdered thyme and then add the crab flakes. Let simmer for a few minutes, pour over some good cream, let boil and reduce to half; before serving add three ounces sweet butter, salt and cayenne pepper to taste. Serve on dry toast and boiled rice on the side.

As a Garnishing, Our Special Service

Hard boiled eggs, chop yolks and whites separately, chopped walnuts, ground powdered Bom Bay-Duck, Bengal chutney.

OYSTER AND FROG LEGS, FAIRMONT

Boil some eastern oysters in their own liquor, skim and drain. Season the frog legs with salt and pepper and prepare the cream of two cups of cream, beaten in with three yolks raw eggs; chopped fine chives and parsley; three ounces of sweet butter and the juice of one lemon. Take sweet butter and let simmer and add a few finely chopped shallots; add the frog legs and fresh mushrooms; steam together for a few minutes. Add one glass white wine, let cool so as to evaporate the acid of the wine, add one cup soup stock, let boil down to half before serving; add oysters and the preparation of cream mentioned above without boiling. Season to taste and serve on dry toast.

FROG LEGS DUGLEVA

Peel ripe tomatoes, press and chop; fresh parsley chopped but not too fine; salt and pepper frog legs. Let simmer, add one chopped onion in butter; pour in the frog legs; let cook together a few minutes;

WORLD FAMOUS CHEFS

pour over the tomatoes and parsley. Reduce the amount of sauce to half. Before serving add three ounces sweet butter.

LOBSTER GOURMANT

Prepare a mixture of chopped fine whites of celery (tender), fresh raw carrots, two shallots and young onions in proportion; one bouquet of parsley, laurel leaves, thyme. Take the meat of lobster, saute in butter, add the mixture; pour over a small glass of cognac or white wine. Let simmer, then cool so as to evaporate the acid in the wine, mix two peeled and chopped tomatoes; add the bouquet, let boil; add one cup of cream; reduce to half. Before serving add three ounces sweet butter. Season with salt and cayenne pepper and serve on dry toast. Take out bouquet.

MUSHROOMS IN RED WINE

Peel and clean carefully nice fresh mushrooms, chopped shallots and white part of young onions; take butter and simmer the shallots and mushrooms in it for a few minutes; add a heaping spoonful of flour, cover with good burgundy wine. Let cook and reduce to half. Before serving add three ounces sweet butter, one teaspoonful of Anchovie sauce, chopped parsley, salt and cayenne pepper. Serve on buttered toast.

PEACH FLAMBEES

Peel some nice fresh peaches by scalding in boiling water. Boil them in water and sugar, vanilla flavor, until tender. Make a nice purre of ripe strawberries; drain off two-thirds of the syrup; pour over the peaches the strawberry puree; add a glass of genuine kirschwasser and set on fire.

SQUAB CHICKEN NELSON

Mince a large onion, parboil for a minute. Soak in water, one cupful of Creole rice. Have a nice tender squab chicken cut in six; salt and pepper well. Put two ounces of butter in chafing dish; add the chicken and onion. Steam it for ten minutes; add the rice and cover whole with good cream. Let cook until done, about forty-five minutes.

THEIR CHAFING DISH SPECIALTIES

SWEETBREADS LORRAINE

Take parboiled calf sweetbreads, cut into pieces a quarter of an inch thick. Put two ounces of butter in chafing dish, add sweetbreads, salt and pepper. Let simmer for a few minutes; add two chopped shallots quartered hearts of artichokes, fresh mushrooms and parboiled scooped small balls of raw potatoes; one glass of white wine and plenty of chopped parsley. Let simmer slowly for forty-five minutes.

POACHED EGG MILANNAISE

Have fresh mushrooms smothered for a few minutes in butter; add peeled and diced fresh tomatoes, ground thyme and bayleaf, a little garlic, salt and pepper, one teaspoonful of meat extract. Add freshly cooked macaroni and grated parmesan cheese. Before serving put poached egg on top.

 # WORLD FAMOUS CHEFS

OTTO GEUTSCH
CHEF DE CUISINE
HOTEL WINDSOR
Montreal, Que. Canada

Mr. Geutsch has been at some of the finest hotels in France, the Hyde Park, London; Cafe Royal, London and also Delmonico's London. The famous chef Monsieur Coffier of the Ritz-Carlton sent him to the Cafe Martin of New York City; later he was at Cafe de la Opera, New York City. While in New York he was awarded five first prizes at the Annual Culinary Exposition and in 1912 received a Medal of Honor by the French Government.

GRENOUILLES SENORITA
(Froglegs Senorita)

Put frog legs into saucepan with piece of fresh butter, chopped shallots, salt, pepper, a little white wine and cook to the point; thicken with cream sauce and finish off with a thickening of egg yolks and cream using one yolk for each person, juice of one lemon, chopped fresh mushrooms and pimentoes which also have been cooked in butter and white wine. Sprinkle with chopped chervil and chives, before serving in a chafing dish.

EMINCE DE VOLAILLE ANNA HELD
(Minced Fowl, Anna Held)

Saute cooked and diced white meat of fowl in butter, fresh mushrooms, chopped shallots, salt and paprika. Deglaze with Cognac or Madeira and little cream, one spoonful of chicken stock, thicken sauce with two yolks of eggs and butter strained, and add this to the rest. Mix well and serve in a chafing dish with a julienne of pimento and truffle sauted in Madeira.

ROGNONS D'AGNEAU MARCHAND VIN
(Lamb Kidneys, Wine Merchant Style)

Figure on three lamb kidneys for each person, chop fine, pepper, salt and fresh mushrooms put in saucepan with butter on a quick fire. Add chopped shallots, little claret and some demiglaze and reduce to one quarter. Thicken with a piece of butter and a spoonful of flour by continuous stirring. Add then a little more butter and fresh ground black pepper, then the kidneys. Serve in a chafing dish very hot and besprinkle with chopped chives before serving.

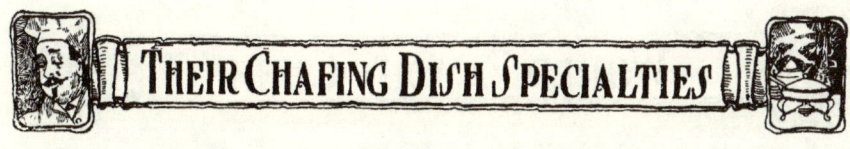

THEIR CHAFING DISH SPECIALTIES

EMINCE DE RIS DE VEAU MIKADO
(Minced Calf Sweetbreads Mikado Style)

Chop calf sweetbreads fine and saute in butter with a few shrimps, fine chopped shallots, season with salt and paprika, a little cognac and Marsala; add a peeled and quartered tomato, a little cream, chicken stock and the usual thickening of yolks of eggs and butter. Season well and serve in chafing dish with slices of truffles (sauted in Madeira) and a bouquet of green asparagus tips placed in center of chafing dish.

O. Gentsch,

PETER BONA
CHEF DE CUISINE
HOTEL
CHAMBERLAIN
(Old Point Comfort)
Fortress Monroe, Va.

Mr. Bona's history since he arrived in this country is brief: three years at the Waldorf Astoria, New York City, in various capacities in the kitchen.

SWEETBREADS A LA BILL EN CHAFING DISH

Four veal sweetbreads diced, eight good sized fresh mushrooms, three fresh tomatoes peeled. Cut in small squares one cup chicken broth, let simmer for fifteen minutes; add salt and pepper. Serve on toast.

FRESH CRAB FLAKES A LA ADAMS

Two pounds fresh crab flakes, three green peppers, six fresh mushrooms, one-half pint sweet cream, one tablespoonful paprika, tablespoonful salt, little grated nutmeg, let simmer for ten minutes and add yolk of three eggs well beaten. Serve in chafing dish with toast.

ESCALLOPS D CAPON A LA BONA

Dice two breasts of capon boiled, three sweet red peppers, two truffles sliced, one pint sweet cream, salt and pepper. Let simmer for ten minutes. Serve in chafing dish, with toast.

Peter Bona

WORLD FAMOUS CHEFS

JULES EDWARD BOLE

CHEF DE CUISINE
HOTEL JEFFERSON
St. Louis, Mo.

Mr. Bole was at Hotel Windsor, Saratoga Springs, N. Y., Hotel Metropole, New York City; Southern Club, New York City; Auditorium, Chicago; St. Louis Club and Mercantile Club, St. Louis, and the Planters Hotel, St. Louis.

CAPON AND LOBSTER NEPTUNE

Take boiled capon and lobster and cut in dice; saute in a saucepan with glass of good sherry and three or four spoonsful of chicken stock, some oysters and slices of truffles. Finish off with double cream and good fresh butter. Serve in a chafing dish with slices of toast on the side.

GRENOUILLE ET CRAB GRENOBLOISE
(Frog legs and Crab Grenoble Style)

Blanch a few frog saddles and bone them; add three or four crabs the same way. Pass through cream and flour and saute in pan with good butter from six to eight minutes. Serve in a chafing dish with noisette butter added which consists of butter, lemon juice and chopped parsley. Season in proportion.

HUITRES EN OMBRELLE
(Oysters in an Umbrella)

Take three to four fresh mushrooms well cleaned; put in a saucepan with butter and arrange in a crown shape around the mushrooms. Blanch with snail butter on top and fresh breadcrumbs sprinkled over the whole and put in oven for ten or twelve minutes. Serve in chafing dish with fried parsley. Season to taste.

MINCED CHICKEN JEFFERSON

Take breast part of a boiled chicken and mince fine; fresh mushrooms sauted in Madeira, cut same way; put in a saucepan with a piece of butter, add chopped green peppers, pimentoes and truffles. Finish off with double cream and serve in chafing dish with slices of toast.

THEIR CHAFING DISH SPECIALTIES

RAGOUT FIN QUATRE SEASON
(Fine Stew a la four Season)

Rooster kernels, coxcombs blanched, fresh mushrooms, sweetbreads in dice, quenelles and truffles, and finish off like Lobster Newburg in chafing dish. Toast on the side. Season to taste.

Jules Edouard Bôle.

ADRIAN DELVAUX
CHEF DE CUISINE
HOTEL BALTIMORE
Kansas City, Mo.

Mr. Delvaux started in at the Grand Hotel in Rheims, France, and thence to the Bristol Hotel in Paris. In this country, at the Chicago Club, Hotel Congress and Annex, Chicago and at the Auditorium Hotel, Chicago. He has been at the Hotel Baltimore for five years, where he has made the Baltimore famous for its cuisine.

MINCED CHICKEN BALTIMORE IN CHAFING DISH

Take the breast of a boiled fowl, cut into thin slices one and one-half inches wide; add one-fourth pound boiled Virginia Ham sliced the same, three good sized cepes sliced; put in saucepan, add one and one-half pints rich cream and bring to a boil. Then take the yolks of three eggs, add a dash of Rhine wine, two ounces creamery butter, beat well together then add same to chicken mixture; stir until it thickens, remove from fire and put in chafing dish; season with salt and white pepper to taste. Serve with fresh toast.

LOBSTER BALTIMORE IN CHAFING DISH

Put in a saute pan some butter, chopped shallots, sliced fresh mushrooms and saute for two minutes; then take two live lobsters, cut into one and one-half inch squares, saute for five or six minutes over a brisk fire; add one glass brandy, two chopped peeled tomatoes and demi-glace; cook for ten minutes; add juice of two lemons and glass of good claret and chopped chives. Serve in chafing dish.

N. B.—Fresh shrimp and live soft shell crabs may be prepared in like manner.

 # WORLD FAMOUS CHEFS

CRAB MEAT BALTIMORE IN CHAFING DISH

Put a piece of butter into saute pan, add the crab meat, some oyster crabs, minced mushrooms and truffles; saute together for a few minutes. Season with salt, paprika, one pint boiling cream; thicken with hard boiled egg yolks. Stir until thick, add a litlle brandy. Serve in chafing dish.

N. B.—Boiled lobsters may be prepared the same as crab meat.

A Delvaux

Their Chafing Dish Specialties

ARTHUR TAYLOR
CHEF DE CUISINE
HOTEL RAYMOND
Pasadena, Cal.

Mr. Raymond is Chef at the Hotel Raymond, Pasadena, Cal. during the winter season, and at the Ocean Side Hotel, Magnolia, Mass., during the summer seasons.

VENISON STAKE
(Hunters Style en Blaizer)

Cut steak one and one-half inches thick from thick part of leg of venison. Put in chafing dish with two ounces butter; pepper and salt to taste. Cook rare with full heat (dry). When nearly done or about five minutes, add one gill port wine, one ounce currant jelly, two ounces of butter, dash of Worcestershire sauce. Serve.

Note—Serve with fresh mushrooms, lintals or julienne potatoes if desired.

MUSSELS A LA MARINIERRE EN CHAFING DISH

Select two dozen mussels; wash very clean. Place mussels with two ounces butter in chafing dish, cover up tight, simmer three minutes; chop three shallots, a little chives and chervil; add to the mussels one-half gill white wine. Let simmer for two minutes. Remove mussels from shells and put back in sauce. Stir in two ounces of butter. Serve with toast.

Arthur Taylor.

WORLD FAMOUS CHEFS

BEN E. DUPAQUIER
CHEF DE CUISINE
HOTEL ARLINGTON
Santa Barbara, Cal.

Mr. Dupaquier's first position was in The Pendennis Club, of Louisville, Ky. Later at the Gault House, Louisville, the Missouri Athletic Club, the Mercantile Club and the New Jefferson Hotel of St. Louis; the Jonathan Club and the California Club, Los Angeles and the Hotel Maryland, Pasadena, Cal

VEAL SWEETBREADS AND FRESH MUSHROOMS A LA DUNN

Four blanched sweetbreads, twelve fresh mushrooms, sliced and one green pepper cut julienne. Saute in butter five minutes, then add one cup sherry wine. Reduce to one-half. Season with salt, paprika and nutmeg. Beat two cupsful of cream with four yolks of eggs. Shuffle about until thick. Serve in chafing dish.

LOBSTER A LA ARLINGTON

Meat of two small lobsters cut in one inch pieces, two sliced truffles and four artichoke bottoms sliced. Saute in butter five minutes; season with salt, cayenne pepper and nutmeg; then add a tablespoonful Madeira and same of brandy. Reduce to one-half. Beat a cupful of cream, and a half cup of milk with five yolks of eggs; add to the lobster and shuffle about until thick. Serve in chafing dish.

Ben E. Dupaquier

Their Chafing Dish Specialties

JOHN CHIAPPANO
CHEF DE CUISINE
AUDITORIUM
HOTEL
Chicago, Ill.
Mr. Chiappano has been with some of the finest Hotels in this country and Europe.

EMINCE OF CHICKEN A LA AUDITORIUM

Cut peanut ham in small strips, saute in white wine, add eminced chicken with cepes and pimentoes; thicken with cream and yolks of eggs with melted butter; serve in chafing dish. Garnish with glace viande.

SWEETBREADS SANS JENE

Take heart sweetbreads, place in pan with butter, add fresh mushrooms; thicken with cream and yolks of eggs; serve in chafing dish with sherry wine and sliced truffles.

FROG LEGS A LA NICOLO DEILAPI

Place frog legs in pan with butter, saute for five minutes, add scallops and oyster crabs; thicken with cream and yolks of eggs; serve in chafing dish with chopped chives and sherry wine. Serve toast on side.

LOBSTER MERRY WIDOW

Place some butter in pan, remove the meat of two lobsters, saute with mussels and oysters. Thicken with cream and yolks of eggs, add cognac; serve in chafing dish with sliced truffles, chopped parsley and red pepper on top.

John Chiappano

www.ingramcontent.com/pod-product-compliance
Lightning Source LLC
Chambersburg PA
CBHW051718040426
42446CB00008B/950